THE *Last-Minute* SUNDAY SCHOOL TEACHER

Cover design by SETTINGPACE

The Standard Publishing Company, Cincinnati, Ohio
A division of Standex International Corporation
Text © 1997 by Cliff Schimmels
All rights reserved
Printed in the United States of America

04 03 02 01 00 99 98 97   5 4 3 2 1

ISBN 0-7847-0477-5

THE *Last-Minute* SUNDAY SCHOOL TEACHER

Cliff Schimmels

STANDARD
PUBLISHING
Cincinnati, Ohio

Contents

Good
Teachers
Pressed for
Time

10:45 pm

SUN MON TUE WED THU FRI [SAT]

Saturday night. Less than fifteen hours before Sunday school. You haven't even looked at the lesson yet. And you're the teacher!

Here you sit—a Bible in one hand; a quarterly and commentary in the other; guilt oozing from every pore; and panic coursing through your veins.

You know better, and every week you promise to do better. But here it is, another Saturday night with the same old story. You've been to all the workshops, and you've heard those Christian education experts explain the process. In a perfect world, Sunday school teachers start on Sunday a week early. They read the text, ponder the implications, and begin research. Throughout the week they gather data, plan activities, develop, and rework. On Saturday night, they sleep restfully, rise refreshed, and go to Sunday school with confidence and polish.

But that's in a perfect world, and you don't live there. Through the week, momentary reminders that you aren't preparing flit through your mind. You convince yourself that you have reasons. After all, you are busy. Work takes a lot of time. The company is downsizing, and you have to pick up hours of overtime. The children are involved with so many activities that you are constantly running here and there, trying to be the best parent you can. Somehow the whole week just gets blown away with thousands of little urgencies that demand immediate attention and problem solving. Isn't it amazing? Our lives are cluttered with time-saving gadgets of every sort, yet we still don't have any free time.

Once Saturday night comes, the Sunday school lesson becomes the immediate urgency. "Why couldn't I have found a few minutes before now to at least look at the topic and text?" you ask yourself—again. Guilt clutters your thinking. Were those reasons or lame excuses? Are you giving something as significant and even critical as Sunday school teaching the time and respect it deserves? Perhaps it would be better for everyone if you would just quit and leave the teaching to those who do start preparing on Sunday the week before.

But you hang in there. For one thing, you enjoy teaching. Despite the fact that you are always under pressure, you feel rewarded. You think you are seeing some growth. Students are commenting favorably. And when you are finished on Sunday morning and you reflect, you feel rather good about the way it went.

Well, if it's any consolation, you are not alone. Throughout this country and throughout the world, thousands—maybe even millions—of Sunday school teachers are sitting right now, hovering over their materials, racked with guilt and panic, scurrying for a Sunday school lesson for tomorrow morning. Some did follow the experts' advice and finished long ago, but they aren't the majority. You last-minute, urgency-bound creatures are the heart and soul of Sunday schools in this country. Let this book encourage you and offer a few suggestions to help you relax and be an effective teacher.

Chapter 1

God Uses Our Efforts for His Good

- Your efforts are worthwhile and may be life-changing
- God can turn your "meager" efforts into spiritual victory
- Jesus is the master teacher

'm not here to judge whether you are the best Sunday school teacher you can be. That is a matter between you and God. But I want to assure you that you can be valuable for the kingdom, even preparing in thirty minutes the night before class.

Not long ago I spent the evening with a pastor of a large church. He was a pleasant man with a quick smile and a twinkle in his eye. Partly because he was such good company and partly because he appeared to be a man of God, I asked him about his boyhood, half expecting to hear the story of a prodigy called to preach at four and ordained at twelve.

"My parents took me to church," the pastor told me, "but my friend and I caused so much havoc that they kicked us out of Sunday school. So when we were ten years old, my friend and I became a Sunday school class all our own. They sent Mrs. Marshall in to teach us. We figured we would run her off just as we had other teachers before her, but it didn't work out that way. Because of her gentle nature and her ability to love us despite how we acted, we both found Jesus that year."

"What became of the other boy?" I asked this successful minister.

"He's a missionary down in South America," he reported.

Be assured. God uses Sunday school classes and Sunday school teachers to reach people with the truth and to change lives to follow Him and His purpose. Even when we aren't as prepared as we need to be; even when we least expect it, God has the power to turn our meager efforts into spiritual victory.

A few years ago I was driving in another state when my car sprang a gas leak. Being something of a mechanical moron, I looked on the positive side. "It's probably my rear valves," I muttered, "and it will cost a bundle to fix."

© Tim Liston

"Larry, pick up! I've got the flu and I need you to teach on Revelation 17 for me this morning!"

With that attitude, I pulled into the parking lot of a rather run-down garage. The mechanic, smelling of tobacco and beer and using language unfamiliar in polite company, came out to assess the damage. I have never felt more helpless standing there at the mercy of this man who didn't seem to hold my value system.

He immediately went to work, took off the fuel pump, replaced a small gasket, charged me a piddling amount, and apologized for the inconvenience.

Somewhat startled, I thanked him for his integrity.

"Well," he said rather nonchalantly, "it's like my Sunday school teacher always said, 'Do unto others as you would have them do unto you.'"

They don't all become missionaries and noted ministers. Some of them might even seem a little rough around the edges, but God is still using you and your Sunday school lesson to get a message across to your students that they aren't going to get anywhere else in our society.

Be assured. You can be a good teacher, even with your preparation schedule. Don't relegate yourself to second-rate. Call these what you wish—tricks of the trade or practical suggestions—there are some techniques to make your preparation time more effective. If you teach small children, you will need to find another book to study. But if you teach a class with people somewhere between the ages of nine and ninety, this book should give you a tip or two.

As you can tell, the book is small. After all, if you're too busy to prepare your lesson, you're too busy to read a long book about it! However, if reading this book whets your appetite and you want to read more about the subject, let me recommend my favorite four books on teaching theories—Matthew, Mark, Luke, and John.

There is a reason why Nicodemus called Jesus "teacher." Jesus was the master. He was the master of relationships—in dealing with students, responding to their needs, and making his lessons fit their anxieties.

But he was also a master of teaching methods. Jesus excelled at holding a crowd, coming up with perfect illustrations, and asking just the right questions to make his listeners think their own way into learning. Three years in the classroom called the world and people are still talking about his lessons, twenty centuries later.

As a Sunday school teacher, you have quite a history to follow. Be assured that the master teacher is cheering for you.

Form Your Philosophy— Everything Flows From That

10.45 pm

SUN MON TUE WED THU FRI (SAT)

Our journey to efficient preparation and effective lessons begins by asking a couple of philosophical questions.

Don't panic! That's not nearly as scary as it sounds. You probably already have a philosophy of education. It's that little voice that dictates to you every time you make a decision. What do you include in tomorrow's lesson? How do you explain this point so that it will make a lasting impression? How do you keep those two boys from picking on that girl? How do you get that every-now-and-then couple into regular attendance?

These are philosophical questions. And your responses come out of your philosophy of education. It's more than just, "Oh, well, I make a decision based on what I think will work." Let me illustrate.

Perhaps you are the teacher of a group of women who have become widows in the last year. How would you structure your class? Lecture? How would you arrange the chairs? Neat, front-facing rows? No, I don't think you would do that. You instinctively know that these women need to be in touch with one another, helping and encouraging each other in a circle of people who care about them. This realization reveals something about what you think of people: how they learn; why they learn; why they come to Sunday school; what's the proper way to treat them.

That's your philosophy of education. The clearer you are about it, the more consistent your decisions and the more effective you will be. So now let's ask two philosophical questions: What is teaching? and, Why do people come?

Chapter 2

What Is Teaching?

- Teaching is one person relating to another
- An effective Sunday school teacher knows the Lord, cares for people, knows the Bible, and knows something about teaching methods

About a million times a week, Sunday school superintendents around the world hear the age-old excuse, "Oh, I could never be a teacher; I can't make a speech." How misguided! Let's get one principle straight right now. Teaching is not making a speech. Teaching is one person relating to another.

"Whoa!" you say. "I'm not sure about that. Isn't that a bit open-ended? What about content? What about presentation?" I agree. The definition is incomplete. But we start here because this definition emphasizes the paramount characteristic of teaching—the relationship between teacher and student.

You may have a golden tongue that can spit out silver nuggets. You may be the master of fancy footwork and the king of audio-visual technology, but unless you can relate all of these techniques to that student sitting in the right-hand corner of the back row, there won't be much learning going on in his chair. And Sunday school is about learning, not teaching.

Just to demonstrate this, let me give you a test. Think about your own eighth-grade Sunday school experience for a moment. Go ahead! Call up those wonderful memories that have had such an impact in shaping you. Now, answer three questions.

1. What company published the material you used that year?
2. What book or books of the Bible did you study that year?
3. Who was your teacher?

How did you do? If you are a typical adult, you scored thirty-three percent on that little test. You got the last question right. And that's my point. The one thing you remember after all these years is the teacher. In twenty years, the one thing your students will remember is you, regardless of how good your lesson is tomorrow.

Now don't get totally discouraged with that line of thinking. You do remember more from your eighth-grade Sunday school class than just your teacher. Tucked away in the recesses of your mind and soul are bits of information, concepts, and insights that influence how you read the Bible, how you treat people, and even how you worship. But all of that is deeply intertwined with the character and personality of the teacher. It has been said, "They won't care how much you know until they know how much you care."

Based on that principle, what are the characteristics of an effective Sunday school teacher?

An Effective Sunday School Teacher Loves the Lord

This is the foremost trait, and it should be immediate and obvious.

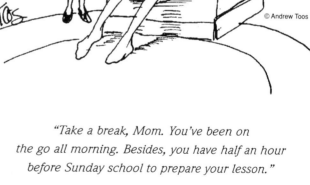

© Andrew Toos

"Take a break, Mom. You've been on the go all morning. Besides, you have half an hour before Sunday school to prepare your lesson."

I know a man who once was an excellent junior boys Sunday school teacher. He had a combination of solid knowledge and good teaching skills, and the boys seemed to respond to his teaching. But one day this role model had an affair with a much younger woman, divorced his wife, and deserted his children. That one selfish act was so powerful that it completely contradicted anything positive the teacher had accomplished. Remember, your lesson and your life are one in the same; your students cannot comprehend them apart from each other.

An Effective Sunday School Teacher Cares for People

You teach because you want people to learn. You know that the material of the Bible is profitable to abundant living. You want your students to experience the joy of knowing Christ, and you want them to know the freedom of submitting to him. Have you ever noticed that many effective Sunday school teachers get discouraged? That's because they care. If they didn't care about their students, it wouldn't matter to them whether they taught well or not.

An Effective Sunday School Teacher Knows the Bible

The Bible is the textbook. It is the content. To be an effective teacher, you don't have to be the world's greatest Bible scholar, but you do need to know that the Bible has the answers, and you need to know how to teach people to find those answers.

An effective Sunday school teacher knows something about teaching methods. They know their students well enough to select teaching styles suitable to their students' learning styles. This book will help you with this.

Chapter 3

Why Do People Come to Sunday School?

- People come to Sunday school to belong
- Know your students' names
- Look at everybody during the lesson
- Include prayer in your class session

To be effective, you need to decide why people get up and make the effort to be at Sunday school week after week. Why do they come? What do they hope to get?

Interestingly, if you ask your students those questions, they probably won't help you very much. "I came to learn the Bible." "I support the church." "I want to grow in the Lord." "My parents made me come." "It's a habit." "I feel guilty when I don't come." "I have no idea."

They truly may not know why they came. They are looking to you, their teacher, to give them purpose. Because this may be a new thought for you, let me offer one reason I think people come to Sunday school, based on almost fifty years of observation: people come to belong. Regardless of the age group you teach, you can see the evidence: the look in your students' faces when they enter into familiar surroundings; the exchanges of greetings; even the ever-popular hitting and slugging common to junior boys. It's all part of communicating a feeling that this is one place where they are comfortable, where they can relax, be themselves, and fit in.

I have philosophically believed in this purpose for Sunday school for quite awhile, but in recent years, I have become adamant about it.

Daily I see the results of crumbling foundations. Families are disintegrating; neighborhoods are breaking up; loyalties are blown into the wind; and in the midst of this are millions of lonely people with an unfilled, inherent human need to belong to something. So they join things. They join dance groups, bridge groups, study groups. They go to the bar where everybody there knows their name. They join gangs, and they join religious groups—Satanic and otherwise—because they need to belong. They may even join a Sunday school class.

This sense of belonging is a vital human need. And it works two ways. We all need to feel that someone cares for us, but we also need to feel that we care for someone.

Let me tell you my favorite story. A little girl was late getting home one evening, and her mother was quite worried. By the time the little girl finally arrived home, the mother was quite angry.

"Where have you been?" the mother asked with a threat in her voice.

"My friend dropped her doll, and it broke," the little girl answered innocently.

"Oh, you stopped to help her fix it?" the mother asked in tones reeking with sarcasm.

"No," the little girl answered calmly, "We couldn't fix it. I stopped to help her cry."

That's why I go to Sunday school. I want to know whom I can depend on to help me cry when crisis comes. Look at Romans 12:15: "Rejoice with those who rejoice; mourn with those who mourn." I call it "the ministry of hanging around." And we all have a deep need to both receive and give. Just as I need somebody to help me cry, I also need to feel that there are people who need my tears when crisis comes to them.

Let's put together two rather obvious facts. People need to belong, and people are lonely. With that in mind, I am now going to say something that won't win me any friends among some pastors and church leaders. I don't mean to be controversial, but for the sake of effective ministry, I feel that I must state my observation. Here it is, take it or leave it. No one belongs to church.

Isn't that a shocker? But I'm confident that I am right. People have membership in church. They come. They worship. They listen. They participate. But they don't get the sense that they belong. Church is too big. Belonging has to be found in smaller groups. Some people find it in the choir. Some in the youth group.

Some in ladies' ministry. But no one belongs to the church. People who belong belong to something within the church. Sunday school is one of those places.

Through the years, I have watched this principle confound Christian education experts. Have you ever seen a church try to go through some kind of mandated Sunday school reorganization? "Let's break up those old classes," somebody reasons. "Get people into their proper age groups." "Get them into special interest groups." "Have the people get acquainted with some new classmates." "Aren't they tired of going to Sunday school with the same old people?"

It all sounds reasonable and looks good on paper, but it doesn't work. The reason people continue together in Sunday school is that the sense of belonging is more important to them than anything else in the whole enterprise. It is comforting to sit among folks who know my history when I raise my hand for unspoken prayer requests.

For you as a teacher, that's good news. It helps you evaluate yourself, and it helps you plan lessons. Let's face it. You can stay up until 2:00 a.m. planning the most profound and appropriate biblical discussion anybody has ever seen; but for fourteen-year-old Ellen, the defining point of success was whether she felt relaxed and accepted during class. It doesn't matter how well you teach if fifty-year-old Frank whose daughter has AIDS leaves your class feeling alone with his burden.

So how does acknowledging your students' need for belonging have any bearing on how you prepare on Saturday night? Let's look at three principles.

Know Your Students' Names

"What?" you ask. Here you are poring through a book on how to be a better Sunday school teacher; looking for sophisticated and time-tested methods and professional, inspiring shortcuts, and I tell you to learn the names of your students? Is this a serious suggestion?

Of course it is. If you don't know your students' names, stop what you're doing and learn them. This is a must. So you have both the Greek and Latin origins of all the verbs in the text. So you have traced all the relevant Scriptures on your topic from Genesis to Revelation. So your illustrations are finer than Swindoll's and Spurgeon's combined. Great! But if you don't know the names of that couple sitting on the third row, they aren't going to learn much today. And if they have been there three weeks in a row and you still don't know their names, forget it. If this is difficult for you, I have suggestions:

- Make nametags.
- Take pictures of everybody and put them on a bulletin board in the classroom.
- Videotape students as they enter, take the tape home, and memorize their names through the week.
- Have the students write something and take it home and read it.
- Go around the room and have the students introduce themselves.

Look at Everybody During the Lesson

In other words, establish eye contact with every student at least once. When a teacher looks at me, I get the idea that the teacher and I are having a one-on-one conversation, even if the teacher is doing all the talking. Interaction is more than talking or doing an activity. It can be as simple as eye contact.

I use a simple technique. After class, I make a list of everyone who was present. I don't do it during class; I wait until the session is over. That way, I have to discipline myself to make sure that

I have looked at everybody at least once. I am convinced that if I look at my students, they will come closer to feeling that they belong.

Include Prayer in Your Class Session

As we have already discussed, this sense of belonging is two-directional. I want to feel that someone cares for me, and I want to feel that I care for someone. For Christians, the greatest act of caring is prayer; thus, prayer is a primary purpose of Sunday school. I come to get prayer help for my own needs and to offer intercessory prayer for the needs of others.

A few weeks ago, I visited a church in another city. One of the teachers asked if I would speak to his Sunday school class. I agreed and began to prepare forty-five minutes of material about my recent mission trip.

Class started, and the teacher asked if there were prayer requests. One man mentioned his son's health. We stopped and immediately prayed for that need. Another man mentioned his wife's job situation. We prayed for that. Other needs were shouted out, and after each one, we stopped and prayed.

Impatient, I studied my watch. First I lost five of my precious forty-five minutes, then ten, and then twenty minutes. When we finally finished praying for everybody's needs, I had only twenty minutes left to inspire the class with the gospel situation in the Ukraine. But when I thought about it, I realized that the first twenty minutes of the session and not the second is what Sunday school is for—a time for people to come together and share their needs in common prayer. No hit and miss, no halfhearted promises.

The Sunday school lesson that day was brilliant, and it had nothing to do with my profound knowledge of the Ukrainian dilemma or my witty means of presentation. The lesson was brilliant because twenty-two men sensed that somebody was caring for them, and they cared enough to stop their busy schedule and bring their needs to God. That's why they had come to Sunday school.

If you are an experienced teacher, you may disagree with my last statement, particularly because it is so definite. What about those people who rarely say much? you ask. Do they

"Enjoy that late movie on TV last night, Mr. Hot Shot Teacher?"

really come to Sunday school to fulfill their need to belong, or do they come for a solid Biblical lesson?

That is a complex question. In my experience, I have found four kinds of people in any classroom setting. There are those who take an active role and participate in the discussion, regardless of whether it pertains to a lesson point or a prayer request. There is a second group of students who participate occasionally but with reservation. The third group sits in class very quietly, watches intently, but rarely speaks. And there is yet another group that just sits there and seems disinterested with the whole thing.

I know these four types. I have studied them for years, and I have come to believe that all of them are involved in their own way. Some people are participating, even though they do not say anything. Don't misinterpret their silence. As the exchanges of request and prayer go about the room, they are sitting there pleased to know someone cares for them and needs their care.

Chapter 4

Teaching People How to Study and Apply the Bible

- Teach people how to study the Bible on their own, rather than the Bible itself
- As you help people learn to study on their own, remember: assume nothing, point out the big picture, model your lesson, and apply your lesson

f my first reason for Sunday school took you by surprise, this one should really raise your curiosity. Don't people come to Sunday school to learn the Bible? After all, isn't that what you do—teach the Bible?

No! You don't teach the Bible, and people don't learn the Bible—not in Sunday school class, not in one hour a week. The book is too big. You will never get through it! You can't even hit the high places in a Sunday school class.

The success of your Sunday school class will not be revealed on Sunday morning. It will be evident on Tuesday night, just before your students turn the light out and lie in bed, alone with their thoughts. Whether they read their Bible or not at that crucial moment depends on their Bible-reading skills and expectations, which they learn in Sunday school.

This is more than just a different way of saying it. There is a big difference between pur-

posefully teaching people the Bible and teaching people how to study the Bible. And that difference affects the way you prepare and present the lesson.

I find this principle refreshing. No longer do you have to get through a mass of facts and material Sunday after Sunday. So you don't get everything in the lesson book "covered"; that's all right if people go home and are hungry to study for themselves.

Three reminders as you help people learn to study on their own: assume nothing, point out the big picture, model your lesson, and apply your lesson.

Assume Nothing

The other day I watched a seventh-grade class study the Civil War. The teacher came prepared with good stories, illustrations, and some really fun activities. The students discussed, created, wrote letters, listened, and answered the teacher's questions. Near the end of the period, after we had been doing this intensive learning activity for almost an hour, one little girl lifted her hand as if she had a burning question and asked, "Who won the war, the North or the South?"

She wasn't being rude and she wasn't stupid. She really wanted to know who won that war. Both the teacher and I had made the same mistake. We had assumed that because these seventh graders had lived in the United States for probably twelve years, they knew by now who had won the Civil War. But when you stop to think about it, why should they know? Where and when would they have gotten that information?

The lesson inherent in this girl's question is particularly appropriate for Sunday school teachers. Most of us have heard Bible stories all our lives. We grew up with them. We know them forward and backward. We don't even remember learning them. And we assume that if we know these stories so well, surely everybody in our class knows them too. What a dangerous assumption.

For one thing, any Sunday school class constitutes the most diverse student body ever assembled. If you were teaching fourth-grade math for example, you could assume that some of those students had slightly better knowledge and skills than others, but you could also assume that all of the students, regardless of ability, have had about the same amount of math instruction along the way. You can assume some similarities.

But not in Sunday school. Some of those same fourth graders were given a Bible for their first birthday, and they've read it so much that the pages of their Bible stick together from the jelly dripped on them. But there are other fourth graders in that Sunday school class who may never have opened a Bible. They don't know the stories. They don't know the exciting tales of giants and slingshots, of clothes that don't wear out, and of days when the sun stood still. Nor do they know that they can live eternally with the God of love.

If you teach adults, the knowledge gap is even greater. Let's suppose you have a lesson from the book of Acts about Paul debating the philosophers in Athens. Some of your students may have read this story in the Greek. Some may remember the scene from history class, and can fill in the details about how the place may have looked and what the people in attendance probably felt and believed. Some students may never have heard this story before, and some may not even be able to find the book of Acts! Your task is to teach them all—teach them so that they understand that the Bible is important to them and that they have the learning skills to master its basic truth. To accomplish this, you have to begin where they are. All

© Jonny Hawkins

learning begins with where the students are now and goes forward from that point, regardless of where that point might be. Don't assume that point.

Learning Begins With the Big Picture

One of the problems with Bible study is that most of us go about it in random fashion, getting knowledge in bits and pieces, skipping around forward and backward, seeing isolated scenes and never fully knowing how they fit in with the rest of the story. The professionally prepared Sunday school lesson is not a solution for this. In fact, it frequently adds to the confusion. Most people who write Sunday school material have a big picture of the Bible, and they know it from beginning to end. In fact, if you look at the curriculum over a three-year period, you will be able to see the wisdom in it all. It's organized and logical.

Yet that couple who comes to your class three times every two months doesn't get that big picture. They just see the lesson for the day, and both their interest in the Bible and their confidence to study the Bible for themselves depends on their ability to see the whole story. An overview of the lesson is critical.

Spend some time thinking about how tomorrow's lesson fits into God's big picture. Make a poster and hang it in the room so that the students can look at it as the lesson progresses. Or, prepare a little sheet and distribute it to your class, making sure that even the incidental students get a copy. It doesn't have to be something elaborate.

Regardless of the technique you decide to use, just knowing the importance of the overview is enough to influence how you prepare and conduct yourself during class. A word spoken in passing relating today's lesson to the big picture can have a powerful effect.

Most Learning Comes Through Modeling

For all our talk of fancy lesson plans, varied methods designed to capture interest and stimulate great learning, and research-proven evaluation devices, most students still learn primarily by watching their teacher. On one hand, that's a scary thought; but on the other hand, it's nice to know.

We can deliberately and purposefully teach people how to study the Bible, but when it's all over, they will probably copy us. Don't be reluctant to tell your students how you study. Talk to them about how you prepared the lesson. Tell them what you read on Tuesday night just before you turn the light off. If you love to read the Bible—if you find joy, comfort, and discipline in its pages—share it with your class. If they go home tomorrow without a single piece of new information but they know that you enjoy reading the Bible, your lesson will have been a great success.

Learning Is Not Complete Until It's Applied

A few years ago, I visited in a home that struck me as a bit unusual. The wife was a successful professional in an industry that required its top-level people to be strong, confident, and forceful. When I first met the wife at her place of business, I was not surprised by her success because she demonstrated all of those characteristics. Then we went to her home where we met her family. The husband was a rather unassuming man with a semi-skilled labor position. The contrast between husband and wife was striking, but in the home the husband took the position of quiet but firm leadership. I spent a pleasant evening in a calm family situation where all members of the family seemed to relax into their individual roles.

The next morning the husband and I awoke early and went out for breakfast at a local truck stop. I couldn't help but tell him how much I enjoyed being with his family and watching the family process work so well.

He smiled a bit and said, "You should have come a few years ago. It wasn't that way at all. There was tension, hostility, and even anger. Then one day during a Sunday school lesson from Ephesians, my wife and I both came away with the same insight. Our family didn't work the way a biblical family was supposed to work. She was too strong, and I was too meek. We decided to become a biblical family. I can't tell you what a difference it has made."

The point is simple. The Bible, although written thousands of years ago, is relevant. When you grab a quarterly on Saturday night and scramble to put together a few things to say the next morning, don't forget that those words, blessed by our omnipotent God, can become a turning point for one of your students. Maybe someone will understand his family better, see a personal sin for its ugliness and decide to give it up, forgive somebody, or accept forgiveness. And every Sunday in a Sunday school class somewhere, someone in the middle of a lesson decides to spend eternity with Jesus Christ. The Bible is a powerful instrument that changes lives.

A Hurried Teacher's Best Friend— The Objective

10:45 pm

SUN MON TUE WED THU FRI [SAT]

The politician stood in front of the crowd and announced, "I am here to convince you that I am the only candidate with the qualifications to fill this office."

The lawyer stood in front of the jury and declared, "During this trial, I will prove to you beyond a shadow of a doubt that my client was nowhere near the scene of the crime when the crime was committed, and is therefore innocent of any wrongdoing."

One day a man went to church. When he came home, his wife asked, "What did the minister preach about today?"

"Sin," the man replied.

"What did he say about it?" she asked.

"Well, I'm not real sure," the husband reported, "but he seemed to be against it."

Do you see the difference? Two of the speakers had an objective. One didn't. The objective is the shortcut to effective instruction. It is the best friend a hurried teacher has.

Every lesson has four components.
- The objective—the aim or purpose.
- The material—the content to be covered.
- The method—the technique the teacher uses to cover the material.
- The evaluation—the device by which the students and the teacher check to see what has been learned.

When we think about teaching, we usually focus on the material. "Today's lesson is about Ephesians 5." "Next quarter, I'm going to teach Genesis." "Last year, we covered the major prophets."

These are logical statements. After all, the Bible is our text, and we need to know which portions we are dealing with. (Incidentally, students in school settings focus on the evaluation. "This class is about three tests and a research paper.")

For the sake of being revolutionary (and to find a shortcut), let's explore what would happen if we began thinking about the lesson by focusing on the objective.

"Today's lesson is about students being able to define their specific roles in their families." "Today's lesson is about students being able to develop Bible-based strategies for dealing with the fears that come naturally through living in today's world." "Next quarter is about students being able to trace the history of the world beginning with Genesis so that they can better understand how God is dealing with us now." "Last year the students developed a timeline of that period of Jewish history when the people were in Babylonian captivity. Thus, the students learned to recognize and explain the signs and dangers of a society separated from God, and can list the steps necessary for reconciliation."

See how revolutionary this approach is? It moves you away from focusing on facts to focusing on the application of facts. It not only gives your teaching a new direction, but it saves you preparation time as well.

Chapter 5

Writing Objectives— When and How

- Write the objective first
- Base the objective on one question: "What do I want the students to be able to do when the lesson is finished that they would not do when the lesson started?" (learner objective)

Write the objective first—at the beginning, the starting point—to save both time and effort.

The Roman historian Tacitus once described the Israelites' forty-year journey in the wilderness as "advancing at random."

Well, that might be satisfactory for the Israelites, but advancing at random is not the way to go on Saturday night with the urgency of a lesson breathing down your back. Before you even open the commentary, before you turn to the right week in the quarterly, determine the direction for your preparation time and for your teaching. Write the objective.

Writing an objective is like going to an ice cream store. Which flavor do you want? Although there are many options available, let's focus our attention on the simplest, the quickest, and perhaps the most effective: the learner objective.

Ask yourself one pointed question: "What do I want the students to be able to do when the lesson is finished that they could not do when the lesson started?" The answer to that question is a learner objective. Let's use James 1:2–8 as an example.

By the end of this lesson, the students will be able to:

- Describe the value of trials in our lives.
- List the steps for dealing with trials.
- Explain the danger of being double-minded.

Look at the progress you have made. Now that you have gone this far, you can teach a fairly effective lesson just from knowing the objectives. But notice how we have written them. The focus is on the student, and what he will gain from the lesson. Contrast this with the teacher objectives prepared for the same lesson:

- We will read James 1:2–8.
- We will investigate the joys of trials.

These objectives tell the teacher what to do but don't lend as much direction as the others.

Learner objectives are easy to write and should give specific direction. When I prepare a lesson, I ask the question we posed earlier: "What do I want those students to be able to do when the lesson is finished that they couldn't do when it started?" I then jot down the answers on my napkin at the restaurant where we are eating on Saturday evening (that's why we don't eat at fancy places—they have cloth napkins). Voila! I'm a third to half finished with my lesson preparation by the time we get home!

Chapter 6

OK, I've Written the Objective—Now What?

- Your objective tells you which material to include
- Your objective tells you which material to exclude
- Your objective tells you which teaching method to use
- Your objective tells you whether the students gained anything from being there
- Clearly communicate your objective to the class

se it! Let your objective tell you how to prepare and how to teach. Your objective has given you a way forward.

The Objective Tells You Which Material to Include

Let's continue using James 1:2–8 as an example. These seven verses are so real, so practical, and so applicable to all of us. How sad it would be for anyone to follow Christ without experiencing the promise of that text! We need to make this passage live in the minds and souls of every student in the class—an awesome responsibility.

But don't panic. Go back to your objectives and choose the Bible texts, the illustrations, and the words you need to leave with the students tomorrow.

For a test run, let's try that third objective: "Explain the danger of being double-minded." I think I know where we can find some material for that. Acts 4:36, 37 tells of Barnabas who had a singular purpose; Acts 5:1–11 tells us the story of Ananias and Sapphira. Now those were a couple of double-minded people for sure. Contrasting Barnabas with Ananias and Sapphira gives the lesson power and a long "shelf life" in the minds of your students. If you want a Bible verse for the day to put up on the board or to have your class memorize, try Revelation 3:15, 16. "I know your deeds, that you are neither cold nor hot. I wish you were either one or the other! So, because you are lukewarm—neither hot nor cold—I am about to spit you out of my mouth." All of those elements combine into a significant learning experience.

How did you think of those Bible references? you ask. Let me assure you that I am no brighter than you, and no better a Bible scholar. Simply, the objective focused my thinking.

"Now here's a good idea for this morning's Sunday school class."

© Erik Johnson

JOHNSON

That's why it's so important to write the objective first.

Your Objective Tells You Which Material to Leave Out

Your lesson preparation book is filled with a variety of Bible verses, illustrations, and thoughts, all of which take off in their own directions. What do you do with all of them? If you include them all, you won't have time to stop and pray for everyone's needs. But if you leave anything out, you will be in some kind of danger from the lesson-planning police who secretly come around to check if you covered all the material! Oh, what to do?

Well, go back to your objective. Your purpose for the lesson was not to cover material but to achieve the objective. Use only the material, the verses, and the collateral readings that will get you to your objective.

Your Objective Tells You What Method to Use

We will talk of methods in Chapter 11, but for now, decide: Are you going to lecture? Ask questions? Divide into small groups? Your response depends on your objective. Once you know what that is, you can make a quick decision about the best method to achieve your purpose.

Your Objective Tells You Whether the Students Gained Anything From Being There

You never really know for sure how effective you are when you base the lesson's value on the encouragement you receive from students. Sure, sometimes students stop after class and say something positive. But did they mean it, or were they just being nice? Some students are appreciative, but may never stop to say a word.

By starting with an objective, you do have a way of telling whether the lesson was worthwhile. If one student can explain the dangers of being double-minded, you know that you have taught and taught well, regardless of whether anybody stops to tell you so.

Be Sure to Communicate Your Objective Clearly

First, tell it to yourself often enough for it to become a natural part of your thought process. Then communicate it clearly to the class. We will talk more about this in the next chapter, but let me encourage you to make sure the students know the lesson's objective before the session ever begins. Just as the objective has given you focus, so it will help the class focus as these truths are embedded in their minds. You are a more effective teacher when you have an objective, and your students are more effective learners when they have an objective.

The Lesson Plan

10:45 pm

SUN MON TUE WED THU FRI [SAT]

Now that you have written your objective, the rest comes easy. It's like fishing. I'm not a fisherman, but I have a friend who is. His secret is, he thinks like a fish. Or, in his words, "If you want to catch a fish, think like a fish." Thus, if you want to teach sixteen-year-old Sunday school students, think like a sixteen-year-old Sunday school student.

For centuries, education experts have stayed awake at night developing formulas to dictate the details of lesson planning. They have done good work, and these lesson plan formulas do save time. Once you have a formula, you just plug in the activities for tomorrow, and presto! You have a lesson plan.

Being a hurried teacher looking for all the help I can get, I like those formulas. They help me save a lot of valuable time on Saturday nights. But the most effective and simplest formula I have found is one based on students' opinions of teaching, measured during the class.

Go to class, sit in the back of the room, and listen to what your students say in their conversations and asides. They will unlock for you this great mystery of the science of learning and the appropriate pedagogical strategies to maximize the process. Plan your lesson according to what they say and in what order they say it. In this section, we'll discuss my findings as I've listened to my students.

Chapter 7

"Help Me Get My Brain In Gear!"

- Use an opening activity to help students get their brains in gear, prepare them to concentrate on the Sunday school lesson, and build enthusiasm for the lesson isten to your students as soon as they walk into your classroom. They may be in Sunday school, but they don't know it yet. They are still bogged down with all the baggage they brought with them from a week's worth of work, school, and home. "We were almost late, and my dad got a ticket." "Mom couldn't find her car keys." "Don't speak to me. I've had a really bad week." "I forgot my Bible, and even in these adult classes, they make you feel guilty when you forget your Bible."

You will also recognize immediately that your students haven't thought about Sunday school once since the last time they were there. You may not have spent much time preparing the lesson, but you can be sure you spent more time thinking about it than most of your students did!

Start the lesson by helping them get their brains in gear and make the transition from their worlds outside of Sunday school to the world where they are now. In fancy teacher talk, we call this the anticipatory set. You can call it the introduction. But the purpose is still the same, and it is an important part of the session.

The good news is that you are probably already doing some form of it. For example, some churches still hold opening exercises. These frequently include corporate songs. As we know, music soothes the savages and gets them ready to learn!

Sometimes an opening song is not a good idea. The other day, I attended a small function; eleven people were going to have a worship service. Recognizing the need to get the group focused, the leader decided that we should sing an opening song. You can guess what happened. The leader and one lady sang, seven others mumbled, and the rest of us sat there in embarrassed silence.

Here are some ideas that may work in place of an opening song:

- Ask for prayer requests and stop to pray for those.
- Have someone in the class explain what you studied and accomplished in the session last week.
- You remind the class of what you studied last week.
- Ask an open-ended question that in some way introduces the material for the day. Let's look at that passage in James one more time. Good opening questions might be, "What kind of decisions do you have to make in a day?" "How do you make major decisions?" "Do you know anyone who has great wisdom? How do you recognize such a person? Now let's look at the text and discover where we can find some wisdom."
- Read an article or clipping from the newspaper that demonstrates a real-life need for the truth of today's lesson.
- Have the students write something. I know this is Sunday school, and we are always reluctant to frighten people with too much "academic" activity, but I think you might be surprised by the effectiveness of an essay question. In recent years, I have asked students in all of my classes—college and Sunday school—to write a brief essay answering a specific question as the opening part of each lesson I teach. Students frequently tell me how much they enjoy and profit from these writing opportunities. Writing is not punishment. It is a tool to help us learn.

Of course, the list above isn't comprehensive, but it will give you some idea of how you can start your class and accomplish three purposes: help students get their brains in gear, prepare them to concentrate on the Sunday school lesson, and build some enthusiasm for the lesson.

Chapter 8

"What Are We Doing Here?"

- Communicate the objective
- Motivate your students by showing them practical application of the lesson in their lives

Would you prefer to teach motivated or unmotivated students? Do you know how to motivate a student? Do you even know what makes a motivated student? Motivation is one of those great mysteries of teaching. We all talk about it, we all wish for it, and we all recognize it when we see it; but we really don't know much beyond that.

But we do know this. Every learner comes to every learning situation with one burning question on his mind: "What will I get out of this?" Your ability to teach that student that day depends on how you answer this question.

Years ago, our Sunday school teachers' response was, "It's in the Bible." We accepted their answer and went on. But we are in a different era. No longer are people expected to go to church. No longer is the Bible the accepted standard against which behavior, values, and morals are set. Couple this with all the other teachers people have in their lives—TV, the

Internet, business conferences, school, or whatever—and you need a better answer. Regardless of whether you teach ten-year-olds, sixteen-year-olds, forty-year-olds, or eighty-year-olds, they still want to know why we are studying this lesson today.

From this, let's put together a definition. Motivation is the ability of the learner to see the applied value of the lesson to be learned. People have specific hopes and hurts. When your lesson fits a specific need, they will learn. For example, a couple having trouble with their teenager will learn from a lesson about children and parents. They are hungry to know what the Bible says about their problem, and they may learn even if your level of preparation is lacking.

To improve your teaching effectiveness, communicate clearly the learning objectives for every lesson. Write them on the board if you have one, or use a flip chart every week and write the objectives on that. If no visual aid is available, at least tell the students in very clear terms what the day's objectives are. And always, always look for the practical value of the lesson to be learned; then communicate it to your class as well.

Every lesson you teach has the potential to be one of great and lasting value. Anticipate the "What's in it for me?" question, and tell your students why you are studying that lesson that day. Help your students see that everything in the Bible is amazingly relevant to our immediate situations every day. As they learn to apply biblical principles to their lives, not only will they be motivated learners in class on Sunday morning, but they will be dedicated Bible students on Tuesday evening as well.

Chapter 9

"Teach Me"

- Decide what method you will use to teach the lesson
- Periodically check with your students to make sure they understand what you're presenting
- Use visuals to help students learn

N ow that you have helped your students get their brains in gear, you've given them the objective, and you've shown them how the study applies to their lives, you are ready to get to the heart of the lesson. The task for you at this point is to decide what method you will use to accomplish your objective. Because that is the subject of the next section, we won't go into detail here, but I will say that there are numerous teaching methods available to you.

One day Jesus was teaching a small group: "Do not let your hearts be troubled. Trust in God; trust also in me. In my Father's house are many rooms; if it were not so, I would have told you. I am going there to prepare a place for you. And if I go and prepare a place for you, I will come back and take you to be with me that you also may be where I am. You know the way to the place where I am going" (John 14:1–4).

Isn't that a great lesson? So full of promise and hope. In one short paragraph the Master gives us the whole gospel—the reason for his coming and the very meaning of our lives.

Have you ever noticed what happens right in the midst of your best lesson? Some student holds up his hand and says something totally irrelevant. That happened to Jesus, too. A student named Thomas said, "Lord, we don't know where you are going, so how can we know the way?"

Isn't that good news? Jesus was the master teacher, the greatest, and even he had students who just didn't get it.

Be assured. While you are delivering the lesson, your students are sitting out there looking at you with great interest and saying to themselves, "I don't get it." By making that statement, I'm not attacking you or your skills as a teacher, but I am recognizing our tendency to make three incorrect assumptions: I said it clearly, they heard every word I said, and they remember every word they heard. None of these are true, so we have to anticipate that somewhere there is a Thomas who has the need—if not the courage—to ask for more clarification. Anticipate that need by checking for understanding and using visuals. Let's examine both methods.

Check for Understanding

Every so often—five minutes, ten minutes, or whatever seems reasonable—stop and ask a specific question of a specific student. "Tom, according to our lesson in James 1, what do we learn from trials?" If Tom cannot answer your question, perhaps

© David Harbaugh

others missed the point as well. Stop, back up, and teach it again, perhaps in a slightly different way.

I am convinced that we don't pay enough attention to this principle. It seems a bit mundane to ask those recall questions. We are eager to get on to deep discussion and real application. But in our rush toward the exciting, we overlook the fact that some students missed a basic point and can't go on. The only way we can discover that is to stop and ask.

A sixth-grade teacher wrote on the board "planned obsolescence." Then she asked if anyone in the class knew the term's meaning. After several seconds of strained silence, one young man ventured a serious response. "Isn't that what we grow into when we leave adolescence?"

Sure it's funny, but that is a teaching problem. How many of your students are just as hazy about such concepts as baptism, salvation, redemption, or sanctification? How will you ever know if you don't stop to check for understanding? The time to do so is while the lesson is actually going on.

Use Visuals

Visuals are concrete illustrations of abstract ideas, and we all need them to help us learn. Paul's epistles would never have made sense to me—regardless of how many times I read them—if I hadn't looked at those maps in the back of my Bible. After studying those maps, I could then read the letters with a definite image in my mind. I had a picture of where it happened and how it happened, and so Paul's instructions to the early Christians made more sense and had more purpose.

You don't have to be a super teacher to design these. Wall charts, simple maps, explanations written on the blackboard, an overhead transparency, a handout you put together yourself—these are some of the most common.

With a little imagination, you can go even deeper. Let's suppose your lesson is James 2:1–4, a passage about favoritism. Call up a few of your students and have them act out those verses as a short skit. You will be amazed at the learning that can take place from such a simple visual. Learning that will last.

Some teachers I know act out the Bible stories themselves. Some even go so far as to make costumes and become the character. I know that would be difficult to do on a Saturday night, but it might be something for future consideration.

I learned another visualization technique from watching my children play a drawing game. They took a yellow pad and a marker and drew pictures to help each other guess song titles. What a neat idea. If you want to increase your effectiveness and save some explanation time, get a yellow pad and a marker and stand in front of your class drawing your points. Watch how that helps your students remember the objective.

Whatever method you use, help your students get the picture. Check for understanding and use visuals.

Chapter 10

"Can I Try That?"

- Shift ownership of the lesson to your students

Your lesson is not complete until your students do something with it. In education jargon, this is called closure. Simply, it is a shift in ownership. To this point, you have owned the lesson's process and concept. Now it's time to shift the ownership to your students. Encourage them to take possession of the concept by using it.

Don't be afraid of this step. Give them an assignment, something specific to do with the objective they have mastered. In children's church, teachers have the children color the wisemen. Other techniques can apply to forty-year-olds:

- Put them in groups of four and have them tell each other how they will use today's lesson.
- Put them in groups of four and have them list the ten most important truths from the book of James.
- Have each person draw a picture depicting James 2:1–4.
- Pose this question to the class, "Imagine for a moment that you are James. How would you finish this sentence: 'True happiness is....'"
- In the closing two minutes of class, have them write a note of encouragement to someone who needs it.

You get the idea. Somehow plan a minute or two at the end of each lesson for the students to do something with what they've learned. Thus, you shift ownership and you give the whole process closure.

Methods

Just for fun, let's make a list of some of the ways we can present a lesson.

- Lecture
- Show a video
- Have a guest speaker
- Present slides and comments
- Have class discussion
- Have everyone read a verse and comment on it
- Have a debate
- Divide into groups and discuss
- Divide into groups and do a project
- Divide into groups and make a class presentation
- Role play
- Dramatize the lesson
- Do worksheets (questions, word searches, crossword puzzles, maps)

Look at what we've done. In just a few moments, we've come up with thirteen different methods. Do you realize that this is enough for you to use a different method for every Sunday in the quarter? If we stayed with this long enough, we could probably come up with fifty-two distinct methods—a different method for every Sunday in the year.

That's the objective of this section—to persuade you to think about what methods are available to you when it comes time for you to teach on Sunday morning. Choosing the right method may be one of the biggest time savers of all, and it will definitely help you be more effective.

If you are a typical teacher, your palms have already grown sweaty just reading this far. Talk of new methods of teaching scares us all—experienced and inexperienced alike. There are two reasons for this. First, we teach the way we were taught. In other words, most of us inherited our methodology. We learned from the generation before us, who learned from the generation before them. We reason, "This is the way we *learned, and if it worked for us, it will work for our students."*

The second reason we tremble at the talk of varying methods is we hate to go outside our comfort zones. We get comfortable with what we are doing, and we are afraid to move out of it. "Forget experimenting. I know I won't like drama. Maybe if I could practice it somewhere else, but I can't. I don't want to fail in front of my class. We'll just keep having group discussion." You have to admit this is negative thinking, so let's see what happens when we think positively.

Give some consideration to the room arrangement. This has great impact on the teaching method you choose, and on the learning that takes place. People feel and act differently in different room arrangements.

Let's consider three arrangements: the classroom look, the boardroom look, and the living room look.

The Classroom Look

If a student walks into a classroom and sees chairs in a straight tow, all facing the front, he will immediately assume that his role in this learning experience is passive. The person at the front of the room standing behind that symbol of authority (a podium or desk), is in charge and has all the answers. A typical classroom look breeds a typical classroom attitude.

One advantage of this arrangement is that it is orderly with few distractions. Any attempt at classroom discussion, however, will not be too successful. People need to see faces and not backs of heads.

The Boardroom Look

In this setting you will find chairs in a circle or square, often gathered around tables. The appearance here suggests that something important is going to happen, but it will be a shared activity. Students know immediately that they are expected to participate.

If the teacher stands outside the circle, the discussion usually takes on a more ordered structure. Responses are directed to the leaders, and the students look to the leader for permission to speak. If the leader sits within the circle, the discussion is usually more spontaneous. Participants respond to each other without filtering all comments back to the teacher.

The Living Room Look

Experts have recently begun to propose the living room look for class discussions. They furnish the classroom with sofas, overstuffed chairs, and soft lights. Participants sit in a relaxed atmosphere and have conversations with each other. Youth leaders who have tried this arrangement have been particularly enthusiastic about what they have been able to accomplish by something as simple as changing the furniture.

Unless your circumstances are unusual, all of these looks should be viable options with just a minimum amount of effort. Your task is to decide which look contributes most to your teaching style.

Warning: This section on methodology is long because there is a wide variety of methods available. But I haven't lost sight of your original purpose for reading this book. You want to find the quickest way to prepare an effective lesson. Choosing the right method—the one suited to you, your class, and your lesson objective—is a major shortcut!

Chapter 11

How Do I Choose a Method?

- Choosing a lesson depends on you, your students, and your lesson

Choosing the appropriate teaching method depends on three factors: you, your students, and your lesson.

You

The best method of instruction is the one you do well. Teaching is such a many-faceted activity that whatever gift God has given you is precisely the gift he wants you to use when you teach. The problem is that you don't discover that gift until you try it. I have known people who lectured for twenty years before they discovered their God-given talent for drama. One of my purposes in this section is to provide you with enough information to give you courage to try something a little different.

Your Students

Just as teachers get into comfort zones, classes get into comfort zones, too. If you decide to experiment with methodology, you may run into a bit of reluctance. Listen carefully to the voices, but don't give up too quickly. For example, teenagers have a moral commitment to the institution of adolescence to say things such as "We've never ever done this before." "This is dumb." "Why don't you just tell us what you want us to know?" But after they have said all of those things, they complain when the bell rings and they have to stop the activity. Adults display the same attitudes but with different means of expression. Don't underestimate your students; they may be more flexible than you think.

Your Lesson

This goes back to the objective. Most days the objective will dictate the appropriate teaching method. In the next few chapters, we'll take a closer look at those methods we mentioned at the beginning of the section.

Chapter 12

Lecture

- Choose to lecture when you have information that your students don't have

The lecture is the most common method of instruction. Notice that the first four methods of the thirteen listed at the beginning of the section focus on teacher talk. Research tells us that in all learning situations, teacher talk fills eighty-five percent of the class time. In other words, we lecture. But there is nothing wrong with that. The lecture method has several proven advantages. Problems arise when we lecture because we haven't thought of anything else to do, if we are not very good at it, or if it doesn't accomplish our objective.

Let's lay down one directive. Lecture is the appropriate method when the teacher has knowledge or insights that the students don't have. It is as simple as that. We lecture because we know more than the students do. We have read the lesson, and they haven't. We have done research, and they haven't. Or, we've had experiences that they haven't.

Some people call lecture the mug-jug approach to teaching. We fill the student's mug out of the teacher's jug. Of course, that is based on the assumption that the teacher's jug is full.

What are the advantages of lecturing? For one thing, it is the most efficient way for you to get information from you to your students. It saves time and energy. You could set up a lab experience of some kind and let them discover it just as you had to discover it. Effective, but time-consuming. Lecture is for teaching and learning in a hurry.

The second advantage of lecturing is that the teacher is in control. You don't have to worry about questions you can't answer, overhead projectors that don't work, or videotapes that break in the middle. When you lecture, you are in charge and you know what to expect.

One morning, I was worshiping at a church in a professional suburban community.

"Please excuse Ellen. She forgot she had a Sunday school lesson to prepare."

© David Harbaugh

Rather than using a lecture for his children's sermon, the pastor chose to use an audience participation device. He had a good message about how the strength of the chain depends on the strength of the individual links. For visual effect, he held up a chain and asked his young audience how it could be used. The outburst of responses pleased the pastor—"To lock your bicycle," "To pull the car when it gets stuck in the snow"—until one little boy spoke loudly, "You can tie it around a dead hog and drag it to the creek." That ended the children's sermon for the day. Do you see why some teachers lecture?

Lecturing has several disadvantages. Although it is the quickest way to disseminate information to your students, it's also time consuming to prepare. Another problem with lecturing is that if it isn't done well, it's boring. Let's face it. Your students listen to many lecturers through the week, from their parents, to their boss, to Chuck Swindoll. You had better be rather good at lecturing if you intend to be effective.

Imagine that you are sitting in the audience. Look at the following characteristics of a lecturer and rank them according to your preference as a listener (1 = most preferable; 8 = least preferable).

____ Has worthwhile information
____ Follows an organized pattern
____ Uses appropriate illustrations or anecdotes
____ Uses appropriate body language
____ Uses effective audiovisual aids
____ Uses acceptable grammar
____ Has a good speaking voice
____ Has charisma

A good lecturer is one who meets the needs of the listeners. Look at your top three choices. How do your lectures rate on these three?

There are several ways you can improve your lectures. First, show the class an outline. Good lecturers are easy to follow. If you wish to improve your lectures, make sure your class can follow you. Write your outline on the board, write it on a transparency, or give it verbally. One of the best methods to hold students' interest is to give each one a copy of the outline with significant parts missing. Thus, the students fill in the missing parts as they listen. What an effective teaching technique this is! Often the students will save these outlines, and when the quarter is over, they will have a complete set of notes.

You can also use audiovisual materials. Common sense tells us that seeing always helps us learn more from what we're hearing. Lecture assigns the responsibility of learning to the sense of hearing. Coupling visual with auditory stimuli has great impact on learning and retention.

We discussed this in Chapter 11, but it's important enough to repeat here. As we said previously, you don't have to be a genius to do this. Write words on the board, cut appropriate pictures out of magazines, buy an inexpensive flip chart to illustrate points as you lecture, use an overhead projector (you can reuse the transparencies), or use flannelgraph. I still remember some of those flannelgraph lessons from thirty-five years ago. If you haven't seen flannelgraph material recently, rummage through your church's storage closet; there could be a wealth of material there for teachers trying to save time. If not, check with your Christian bookstore. You can find flannelgraph lessons for every part of the Bible.

Finally, tell stories. One day God told Nathan, "Go teach King David that he is a sinner." Regardless of how tough you think your teaching assignment is, you've never faced a lesson with any more pressure than that. If you want to know how Nathan handled the assignment, turn to 2 Samuel 12. The teacher told a story, and the king learned his lesson and changed his heart.

That's the point. Effective lecturers tell stories. Again, you don't have to be a novelist or an entertainer. Even a simple account of something that happened to you this week will touch the hearts of your students and make your lesson long-lasting.

Chapter 13

Class Discussion

- Choose class discussion when you want to allow your students to express their ideas and opinions to each other f you believe that your students have good ideas and valuable opinions, then you will want to choose a method that will allow them to express their ideas and opinions to the class. This is class discussion. Let's look at a couple of common techniques for achieving this. These are methods six and seven in the list at the beginning of the section.

Have Everyone Read a Verse and Comment On It

As I travel from church to church, I have observed that this may be the second most common method of Sunday school teaching, particularly in small classes. There are reasons for its popularity. For one thing, it's easy to prepare. You don't have to lie awake on Saturday night wondering what the commentary says or where to find an appropriate illustration. This method also gets everyone involved in the process of teaching. Students get the feeling that the class belongs to them and that they have a role in determining the quality of the experience.

I have seen this method used quite effectively, but there are always a couple of potential problems. For one thing, this method may not reach a common objective. If your objective is to read the Bible verses (teacher objective), this method will work. But if your objective is to get your students to apply these verses to their lives in a significant manner (learner objective), this read-and-comment method may not be too effective.

Another problem is that this method may embarrass some people. You may have students who don't read very well; almost all classes do. You definitely have students who feel that their comments aren't worthy. Be alert and recognize people's anxieties; help them feel a part of the class.

The Debate

Sometimes called the Socratic method, sometimes called the inductive method, sometimes called the discussion or question-and-answer method, this popular form of Sunday school teaching has attracted strong supporters. Although the method requires a skillful leader, it's not nearly as mysterious as it may sound. By mastering a few principles, you may find that you are rather good at leading a discussion.

There are many ways to form a good question. Questions come in several categories depending on the mental skill required to answer. Because Jesus was so good at asking questions, let's look at his example. He asked his disciples, "Who do people say I am?" That is a knowledge-based question. Answering it requires a simple reporting of information. There is a right answer, and there is a wrong answer.

But then Jesus asked, "Who do you say I am?" Do you see the difference between these two questions? In education jargon, we call that second question a higher-order-thinking question. Answering it requires thought, self-analysis, and maybe even a little creativity. There's no way for an outsider to determine whether your answer is right or wrong.

Let's now put your questioning skills to a test. Suppose the lesson for today is from Luke 15, the story of the prodigal son. Look at the following list and decide which ones are reporting questions and which are thinking questions.

1. How many sons did the father have?
2. What happened to the younger son?
3. What happened to the older son?
4. What happened to the younger son's money?
5. What happened when the younger son came home?

6. Do you know anyone like the younger son?

7. Do you know anyone like the older son?

8. Do you think "The Parable of the Prodigal Son" is a good title for this passage? If not, what would be a better one?

9. To whom did Jesus tell this parable?

10. What do you think his purpose was?

Wow! I get excited just thinking about the kind of discussion a class could have with these questions.

Now, you try it. Look at the text for your next lesson. Write three questions of the reporting type and three questions of the thinking type. Once you have mastered the principle, writing good questions is a learned skill. You will improve with practice.

Actually, asking the questions is not as obvious as it may seem. It deserves some thought. Some teachers ask only people who raise their hands. Some teachers try to question everybody. Some teachers ask students when it is obvious that they don't know the answer. You will have to make a decision as to what you are comfortable doing.

There is one principle that will help. Always begin by asking the reporting type questions. Get the students involved in answering before going to the heavier material. If the discussion gets bogged down, go back to some reporting questions to get it started again.

Your response to the students' answers may be more significant to the quality of the discussion than the questions themselves. Most of us have had the experience of being squelched by a teacher's response to something we said in class. Don't do that to your students! Consider the difference in tone among the following:

- "Yes, that's the right answer. Thank you."
- "I like your answer, but have you ever considered—"

- "What else do you have to say about that?"
- "Does somebody else have a response?"

As you can see, the way you answer students' questions will greatly influence the character of the class discussion. This, too, is a learned skill, but it merits some practice. I have seen teachers conduct an hour-long discussion with only three questions and appropriate responses.

Chapter 14

Study Groups

- Choose study groups when you want to help people get to know each other or to get them involved in the lesson tudy groups (methods eight through twelve on the list at the beginning of the section) are appropriate in many situations. They have three distinct advantages: students get acquainted with each other, more people get involved in the lesson, and they are often easy to prepare.

There is no method more effective for getting students to know each other or for helping them feel like they belong than to divide them into study groups for some or all of the class period. Study groups are particularly valuable when class membership is changing and new students are entering.

During a successful class discussion, only half of those present may participate. But a challenging study group project may increase that number to seventy-five or one hundred percent. It is always amazing to watch a seemingly quiet, steady person take over leadership duties during a small group activity.

Finally, it is generally a simple matter to jot down three assignments. Decide how you are going to split the class into groups and put them to work.

I use study group projects regularly. My colleagues and students alike often comment about how creative I am. I wouldn't dare tell them that I use this method because I didn't take time to prepare a lecture!

The small group method is so flexible. You can use it for a portion of the class or for the whole period. You can use a small group activity for the application step after you have presented the lesson, or you can involve small groups in the presentation itself. Let's look at some of the possibilities.

Group Prayer

If your students don't know each other, if you have a large class that necessitates the lecture method of presentation, if you have a large number of prayer requests, or if you just want the students to be active, divide the class into groups and let them pray. I have a personal testimony related to group prayer. I am afflicted with an almost debilitating shyness. I don't like to speak out in crowds unless I am the leader. But I really enjoy getting together with three or four people and joining with them in prayer. There is something reassuring to know that I and these strangers have a common bond through our spiritual Father.

Group Discussion

I have seen teachers divide the class into small groups and instruct them to discuss a point of the lesson. This is a fair technique but not a really good one. This kind of open-ended assignment requires each group to spend too much time finding direction, and often the group doesn't know when it's finished. Members either quit early or take too long.

Group Activity

Study groups usually work more effectively when they have specific direction. You can have all the groups working on the same activity, or you can make specific assignments to each group by simply writing a couple of sentences on a card for the group to work with. For example, suppose you have enough students for three groups to study James 1:2–11. Tell all three groups that they are to draw a picture (you will want to provide paper and pencils) illustrating the truth of these assigned verses. Then give group one verses 2, 3, and 4; group two verses 5, 6, 7, and 8; and group three verses 9, 10, and 11.

Can you see the possibilities in such a project? The students will have to develop a thorough knowledge of the verses, they will have to discuss them, they will have to conceptualize an application, and they will have fun doing it.

And you only spent thirty minutes—tops—preparing your lesson!

Group Presentation

This is usually just an extension of the small group project discussed above. Let's use the same passage (James 1:2–11). Instead of having the groups draw a picture, have them take about half the period planning a drama or a role play illustrating the truth of their verses. Then use the second half of the session to present the dramas.

Sometimes it is a challenge to assign people to groups. Random assignment is easiest, but you may occasionally want to assign groups yourself. You may do this to make sure you get leaders in each group, to help people get acquainted, or to control the noise level.

Here are some other tips to help groups work better. To control disturbance, give full instructions before you let the students divide into their specific groups. Also, stay on your feet throughout the activity. Look in on each group, answer questions, make suggestions, or encourage. Most important, be available. Finally, watch the time. Group work loses its effectiveness when you allow too much time for the task to be completed. If you have to err, err by calling groups to a halt too quickly.

Chapter 15

Written Activities

- Written activities can intensify your students' learning experience

Yes, I know this is Sunday school. Your students don't get grades. But they did come to learn, and if you can contribute to their learning by using a written activity, use a written activity.

Writing is a good—no, one of the best—learning tools. You prove this all the time. If you want to remember something, you make a note. If you want to organize your thoughts or your day, you make a list. If you want to clarify your thoughts, you write your thoughts down. If you are looking for some technique to deepen and intensify the learning experience of your Sunday school class, you may want to examine the virtues of writing activities.

Another use of the written activity is to give the students something to occupy their minds and hands.

"Wait a minute," you protest. "Isn't that busy work?"

Of course it is. You are probably a good enough teacher that you don't need busy work, but I'm not. I still get into those situations where I just don't have the skill to lecture to eleven-year-old boys about the Bible for forty-five minutes. I need all the help I can get. So I use written activities. It calms them down. I'm able to keep peace. And they are convinced that they are learning something.

There are many kinds of written activities. Journaling, or the habit of writing down your thoughts, has become one of the acclaimed activities of spiritual growth. From famous church leaders to people in the pews, those who journal attest to its value in their lives. Journaling one day a week in Sunday school is not the same as journaling seven days a week, but it is a start. Perhaps your students will get the idea and pursue this on their own.

Make the journal entry open-ended. "Spend a few minutes writing down your thoughts for the day." Or make it more structured. "Write a paragraph explaining how you would feel if you were the parent of those two sons in Luke 15."

If your objective is to help your students develop the skill of reading the text on their own, you may want to explore worksheets. Write out some questions that are to be answered from the text. This is really not as difficult as it sounds. With the availability of photocopiers, you can easily put questions in the hands of all students.

Some teachers have students complete worksheets during class time, so this becomes the method of instruction. Others have students prepare worksheets before class and use class time to discuss answers. This latter method will definitely improve the quality of discussion.

If you are creative and want to put a little fun into learning, prepare game sheets such as crossword puzzles or word search games using words or names from today's lesson.

One drawback of written activities such as worksheets or game sheets is that you have to prepare and supply all the materials. And this is Saturday night, remember? You will at least have to supply pens and paper. If you use a weekly journal, you will probably want to keep these stored in the room or with you through the week.

It's Saturday Night— What Now?

- Cliff prepares a lesson step by step— in one hour!

know what you're saying. "Okay, Cliff. I've read the book, I've learned how to write an objective, I've learned how to ask good questions, I know how to arrange my classroom, but—IT'S SATURDAY NIGHT AND I STILL DON'T HAVE MY LESSON! Can you help me? Just this once?"

Well, I know it's a lot to absorb at one time. So on the following pages I've included an outline that shows the steps I followed as I prepared a lesson on Nehemiah 4. All nine steps took just under an hour! I hope this helps you put the principles in this book into action.

Step 1
Time Elapsed: 1 Minute

Find a sheet of paper and make a lesson plan outline form.
A. "Help me get my brain in gear."
B. "What are we doing here?"
C. "Teach me."
D. "Can I try that?"

Step 2
Time Elapsed: 5 Minutes

Read the Bible text—Nehemiah 4.

Step 3
Time Elapsed: 5 Minutes

Think about the people in the class. I won't dwell on any individual for a long period of time, but I will try to think for a moment about each one and his particular joys and sorrows.

- *Roger and Amy are just finishing a week with a child who had chicken pox—the first of three—so they will be homebound for several weeks.*
- *Addie learned last week that her mother has cancer.*
- *Tom got a huge promotion, but it will require him and Lois to move to the West Coast.*

Step 4
Time Elapsed: 6 Minutes

Read the Bible text again, but this time read the devotional reading assigned to the lesson (Nehemiah 9:6–16). As I read, think about the people in the class and look for applied meaning for each.

Step 5
Time Elapsed: 5 Minutes

Write my objectives under Point B of the outline, bringing together class members with the Bible lesson.
The student will be able to:
- *Explain why it was so important to the Jews to rebuild the wall.*
- *Identify their enemies in the project.*
- *List the steps the Jews took to guard against their enemies.*
- *Describe how the Jews gained confidence to complete the job.*

Step 6
Time Elapsed: 3 Minutes

Think about the practical application of the Scripture.
- *The Jews came back to a scene of destruction and devastation. The typical human response would be despair and surrender.*
- *How often in life it is easier to surrender for comfort than to conquer for real joy!*
- *In building the wall, the Jews realized three things:*
  —*The therapy for despair is purposeful activity.*
  —*You never go through despair alone. It's a shared emotion even though we don't always know others are participating in it with us.*
  —*Our relationship with God is a history of blessing. Why should we expect anything else for our future?*

Step 7
Time Elapsed: 6 Minutes

Plan Point A on your outline: "Help me get my brain in gear."
Let's explore some options.

Option One

Read a news article—a story of a college group building a Habitat for Humanity project; a story of a community coming together to clean up a beach; a story about several churches coming together to help a burned-out congregation rebuild their sanctuary.

Questions to consider: Why do people rally around a common project? Were the people of the past more willing to help than those of today?

Option Two

"Think about a time when you were part of a cooperative project. How did you feel as a participant? What is the value of a common goal? What is the common goal of our church? What is the common goal of your family?"

Step 8
Time Elapsed: 23 Minutes

Plan the rest of the lesson and write under Point C ("Teach me") a schedule for the session. It looks like this:

1. Do Point A; use Option Two.
2. Write objective on board (Point B).
3. Read devotional text aloud.
4. Talk about applying the Scripture to life.
5. Distribute reading assignments and have them read aloud:

   Reading One: 4:1, 2
   Reading Two: 4:3
   Reading Three: 4:6–8
   Reading Four: 4:11, 12

6. Stop here and ask a few questions: *What are the Jews trying to do? Who are the adversaries and what is their approach to the Jews' work?*

Do you notice a change in the attitude and actions of the adversaries as the chapter progresses?

7. Have the second reading assignments read aloud:
   Reading Five: 4:6, 8, 12
   Reading Six: 4:13, 14
   Reading Seven: 4:15–18
   Reading Eight: 4:19–23

8. Stop here and ask some more questions: *How do the Jews protect themselves from the adversaries? List all the ways. Does the wall make progress? What are Nehemiah's leadership techniques? Why do you think the Jews were so dedicated to the project?*

9. Have the third reading assignment read:
   Reading Nine: 4:4, 5

10. Stop here and ask some questions: *On what does Nehemiah base his faith to pray? How does God help them?*

11. Now for Point D. Divide the class into three groups. Have each group write daily diary entries for the following people:
    Group One: Sanballat
    Group Two: Nehemiah
    Group Three: A wife whose husband is working and guarding the wall.

12. Have a designated reader read those diary entries. Comment during the reading about how the entries refer to the specific lesson objectives.

13. Ask for prayer requests and pray until the session ends.

Step 9
Time Elapsed: 6 Minutes

Pray for the lesson.

The lesson plan is now complete. I can watch the news, go to bed, and sleep through the night knowing that tomorrow I will be prepared to teach effectively. At this point, you probably have a few impressions:

1. *The lesson plan seems rather simple. Of course it is. I made it that way on purpose. Effective teaching is not nearly as complicated as textbooks make it seem. Planning an effective lesson is not complicated, either.*

2. *Little things like dividing that chapter into reading assignments and writing those assignments on sheets of paper or cards may sound tedious and time consuming, but they aren't. You can do all that in two minutes, providing you have some sheets of paper handy.*

3. *Preparing the point-by-point outline first not only saves valuable planning time; it also gives the lesson direction and coherence.*

4. *Planning always begins with the objectives.*

Cliff's Top 10

If you don't have time to teach Sunday school, you may think you don't have time to read this book. Here's a quick version of my 10 most valuable teaching shortcuts.

1. **Give a one-sentence answer to the following questions: What is teaching? and Why do people come to Sunday school?**

   The answers to these questions constitute your philosophy of education. Out of your own experiences and expectations find the exact sentence that says precisely what you are about. Repeat it to yourself over and over until this thinking is a part of you. Then when you sit down on Saturday night in a fit of urgency, that philosophy will focus your thoughts, your efforts, and even your panic.

2. **Write your objective first.**

   Effective teaching is effective because it accomplishes an objective. If you don't have an objective, you won't know how to prepare, present, or evaluate.

3. **Learn your students' names.**

   Effective teaching is first an effective relationship. Students come to your class to feel that they are in a place where everybody knows their names. The most effective use of your preparation time is to master the names of your students.

4. **Lay the tools out before you start preparing.**

   If you were going to repair a faucet, you would find your tools before you start. The same principle applies to preparing a Sunday school lesson. Although these tools are a matter of personal choice, there are a couple that are absolutely essential: a good study Bible and a one-or two-volume Bible commentary. Some I like are *The Thompson Chain-Reference Bible*, available in a variety of translations, and the two-volume *The Bible Knowledge Commentary* by Walvoord and Zuck.

5. Listen to your students.

The greatest teaching skill is the skill of listening. Your students come to be heard as well as to hear. They have needs and joys, prayer requests and prayer answers. Their needs are as relevant to the purpose of Sunday school as the lesson. A well-prepared lesson is one that is flexible enough to allow students to speak, and addresses the learning needs of your students.

6. Experiment with teaching methods.

Unless you have tried using different presentation techniques, you may be wasting a lot of planning time trying to make yourself fit the method. The efficient way to teach is the opposite. Choose a method that fits you, your class, and your lesson objective. Try several methods. You won't know which ones you have natural talent for until you try them. In the process, you may have to learn a new skill or two, but in the long run, taking time to learn a new skill may be one of the biggest shortcuts of all.

7. Arrange the classroom to meet your needs.

The room arrangement makes a difference in how people learn, and it makes a difference in how you teach. Think about the best design for the objective, the lesson, and the method you plan to use today.

8. Use visuals.

Seeing helps us learn what we're hearing. If you want to maximize learning, surround your students with things to look at. Hang charts, graphs, maps, and pictures on the walls. If you have a chalkboard, write on it. Put your objectives and outline up for everybody to see. Write hard-to-pronounce words and significant points. Draw charts that explain. If you have an overhead projector, use it. If you have neither chalkboard nor overhead projector, invest in an inexpensive flip chart and increase your teaching effectiveness several fold!

9. Tell stories.

The story of what God did for Paul on the road to Damascus is a powerful message. Tell it with enthusiasm. Tell it from start to finish. Cover every detail. Create word pictures that help your students see the place and the action. There is power in the story. The story of what God did for you last week is a powerful message. It may be even more powerful than the story of what God did for Paul because some of your students feel that Bible characters are spiritual heroes, and they know you aren't! Tell your story. Tell it with enthusiasm and boldness. Tell your class how God answered your prayer. Tell your class how God has not answered your prayer and how you are dealing with it. There is power in your story. Tell it.

10. Pray.

Unless you are the smartest person God has ever created, you are not bright enough to teach Sunday school. The task, the responsibility, and the expectations are too big for you to handle. Don't despair. God knows that. James explains how God has made provisions. "If any of you lacks wisdom, he should ask God, who gives generously to all without finding fault, and it will be given to him." (James 1:5). You aren't bright enough to do the job yourself, but you have the whole realm of God's wisdom available to you. Take advantage of that.

Every week in Sunday school classes across this country, teachers show up less than fully prepared, harboring guilt, doubt, and indecision. But they struggle through, and God takes those less than perfect efforts, adds his blessing to the whole process, and accomplishes his purpose in the lives of people. That's the joy of teaching Sunday school. When you ask God to help you prepare and you ask God to help you teach, you never work alone.

The following cartoonists have contributed to this book:

Dick Hafer, page 21
David Harbaugh, pages 51 and 64
Jonny Hawkins, pages 26 and 35
Erik Johnson, page 38
Dik LaPine, page 69
Tim Liston, page 6
Andrew Toos, page 13